PYTHON
KIDS

*LEARN TO CODE QUICKLY
WITH THIS BEGINNER'S
GUIDE TO COMPUTER
PROGRAMMING. HAVE
FUN WITH MORE THAN
40 AWESOME CODING
ACTIVITIES, GAMES AND
PROJECTS, EVEN IF YOU ARE A
NOVICE.*

CHRISTIAN MORRISON

TABLE OF CONTENTS

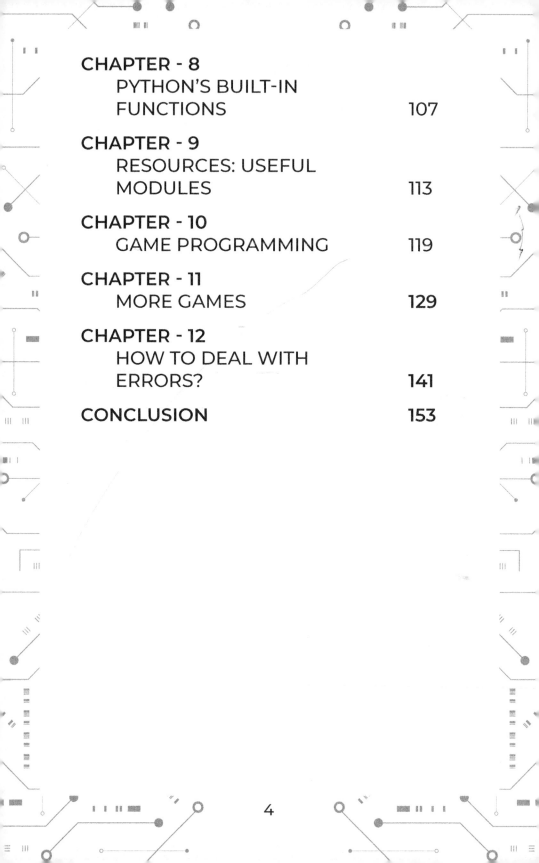

INTRODUCTION

(handwritten: read tomorrow again)

What is coding? Coding is the process of putting together the segments of your data that seem to illustrate an idea or concept. In this way, coding is a way of making abstractions from the existing data in their resources to build a greater understanding of the forces involved.

Remember that it is possible to code any portion of the content of a resource on any number of nodes to show that it is related to each of its concepts or categories.

Why Learn to Code?

The coding of the content of your resources can contribute significantly to your analysis in several ways: *(handwritten: tomorrow again)*

- Coding allows you to gather and view all the material related to a category or case through all its resources. Viewing all this material allows you to review the coded segments in context and create new and more refined categories as you gain a new understanding of the meaning of the data.

- The codification of its resources facilitates the search for patterns and theories. It is possible to browse the encoded content of your resources using queries and search functionality to test theories and find new patterns in your data.

Example: When coding in C the algorithm of the program Add, seen in the Design, something similar to:

```c
#include <stdio.h>
int main ()
{
    int a, b, c;
    printf ("\n first n% number (integer):", 163);
    scanf ("% d", & a);
printf ("\n second n% number (integer):", 163);
    scanf ("% d", & b);
    c = a + b;
    printf ("\n The sum is:% d", c);
    return 0;
```

To encode an algorithm, you have to know the syntax of the language to which it will be translated. However, regardless of the programming language in which a program is written, it will be its algorithm that determines its logic. The logic of a program establishes what its actions are and in what order they should be executed. Therefore, it is convenient for every programmer to learn to design algorithms before moving on to the coding phase.

Programming Languages

A programming language can be defined as an artificial language that allows you to write the instructions of a computer program or put another way. A programming language allows the programmer to communicate with the computer to tell it what it has to do. Many programming languages have invented by man. We can classify into three main types: the machine, low level, and high level.

Machine language is the only one that understands the digital computer. it is its "natural language". Only two symbols can be used on it: zero (0) and one (1). Therefore, machine language is also called binary language. The computer can only work with bits. However, it is not easy for the programmer to write instructions such as:

```
10100010
```

```
11110011
00100010
00010010
```

For this reason, more understandable programming languages were invented for the programmer.

Thus, low-level languages appeared, also called assembly languages, which allow the programmer to write the instructions of a program using English abbreviations, also called mnemonic words, such as ADD, DIV, SUB, etc., instead of use zeros and ones. For example, the instruction:

ADD a, b, c   Add   a, b, c

It could be the translation of the action:

$c \leftarrow a + b$ $C \leftarrow a + b$

This action is present in the Add algorithm of the Design, which indicated that in the memory space represented by the variable c the sum of the two numbers stored in the memory spaces represented by the variables a and b must be stored.

A program written in an assembly language has the disadvantage that it is not understandable to the computer since it is not composed of zeros and ones. To translate the instructions of a program written in an assembly language to instructions of a machine language, you must use a program called an assembler.

An added difficulty to binary languages is the fact that they are dependent on the machine, or rather, the processor, that is, each processor uses a different machine language, a different set of instructions, which is defined in its hardware. Consequently, a program written for a type of processor cannot be used on other equipment that uses a different processor, since the program will not be portable. For this program to work on a second computer, all instructions written in the machine language of the first computer must be translated into the binary language of the second computer, which is a very expensive and complex job for the programmer.

Likewise, since the instructions that can be written in an assembly language are always associated with the binary instructions of a particular computer, assembly languages are also processor dependent. However, high-level languages are independent of the processor, that is, a program written on any computer with high-level language can be transported to any other computer, with small changes or even none.

A high-level language allows the programmer to write the instructions of a program using words or syntactic expressions. For example, in C you can use words such as case, if, for, while, etc. to build with the instructions like:

```
if (n0> 0) printf ("The number% is positive", 163);
```

This translated into English comes to say that, if the number is greater than zero, then write the message on the screen: "The number is positive."

Another important feature of high-level languages is that, for most of the instructions in these languages, several instructions in an assembly language would be needed to indicate the same. In the same way that, most of the instructions of an assembly language, also groups several instructions of a machine language.

On the other hand, a program is written in a high-level language also does not get rid of the inconvenience of the fact that it is not understandable to the computer and, therefore, to translate the instructions of a program written in a high-level language to instructions of a machine language, you have to use another program that is called a compiler.

What Can You Make with Code?

You can do many things with codes. For example, let's see what can be done with JavaScript code.

The things that can be done with Code are very varied, among the most prominent are:

1. You can obtain the information about the browser that the user is using, the version of it, the operating system on which it is running, and even the screen resolution that you have configured on your computer.

2. You can work with pop-up and interactive dialogs created with div elements, instead of pop-up windows, which have stopped being used for security and design reasons.

3. You can create sophisticated menu systems with pop-up submenus that are activated with the user action.

4. Values entered in form fields can be validated before they are sent to the server.

5. You can create navigation trees to make it easier for users to move from one page to another through your website.

6. You can create substitution effects for images controlled by the action of placing or removing the mouse pointer.

7. You can create some animations such as transitions of images and objects from a web page.

8. You can change the position of HTML elements on the web page dynamically or controlled by the movement of the mouse pointer.

9. You can redirect the user from one page to another, without the need for a static link.

10. You can perform some calculations with the values entered in the form fields.

11. You can get the date of the operating system where the web page is running on the client.

12. Sophisticated calendar controls can be created to select a date, instead of being manually entered by users in form fields.

Types of Errors

When a syntax error exists in any instruction of the source code of a program, this error will prevent both the compiler and the interpreter from translating said instruction, since neither of them will understand what the programmer is telling you. For example, if instead of the instruction:

```
printf ("\ n first n% number (integer):", 163);
```

When the compiler or the interpreter reads this line of code, neither of them will understand what prrintf is and, therefore, they will not know how to translate this instruction into machine code, therefore, both will stop the translation and notify the programmer with a message of error.

In summary, syntax errors are detected in the process of translating the source code into binary code. On the contrary that it happens with the errors of execution and of logic that can only be detected when the program is running.

A runtime error occurs when the computer cannot execute any instructions correctly. For example, the instruction:

```
c = 5/0;
```

It is syntactically correct and will be translated into binary code. However, when the computer tries to perform the division:

```
5/0
```

An execution error will occur, since, mathematically, it cannot be divided by zero.

As for logic errors, they are the most difficult to detect. When a program has no syntax or execution errors but still does not work well, this is due to the existence of some logical error. So, a logic error occurs when the results obtained are not as expected. For example, if instead of the instruction:

```
c = a + b;
```

A programmer would have written:

```
c = a * b;
```

Until the result of the operation was shown on the screen, the programmer could not realize the error, provided he already knew the result of the sum in advance. In this case, the programmer could easily notice the error, but, when the operations are more complex, the logic errors can be very difficult to detect.

CHAPTER - 1

GETTING STARTED WITH
PYTHON

What is Python?

Python is a minimalist programming language, which contains a syntax that makes it quite simple. It is an interpreted language, that is to say, not compiled, in addition this serves for all types of development specially to give dynamics to objects in different programs and / or paradigms.

Undoubtedly Python is one of the best options to develop a website, especially when you know the basic elements of language.

Let's see Python what offers us.

Python Features

Before continuing, we will point out some important Python features and why you should learn it.

Minimalist Code

Yes, the code and the simple syntax are perfect for developing websites, facilitating the work and writing of it.

Well Paid

That's right, if you are going to develop a Python website, prepare your bank account, since the benefit you will receive from developing a Python website will be very profitable, as you can see in Medium.

Multiplatform

Python can not only run it in an operating system, so you can take it anywhere, from free operating systems such as Linux and through the already known Windows or Mac, in addition to other devices that have systems based on the aforementioned distributions.

Extensive Libraries

An advantage that comes very well from Python is the number of libraries or libraries you can find to develop.

There is a wide variety of reusable code, from game creation to large websites and quality.

Installing Python

On a PC

If you are using Windows machine, you can follow the procedure below.

Step1. Let us begin by opening up our web browser and going straight to the source. In the address bar, type in www.python.org and you will be greeted by a simplistic website as shown here:

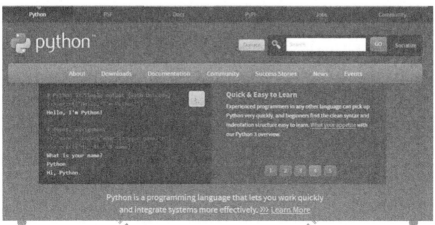

Step2. Mouse cursor over 'Downloads' and the website should be able to detect your platform and present the corresponding version accordingly automatically.

Step3. Click on the button to commence the download.

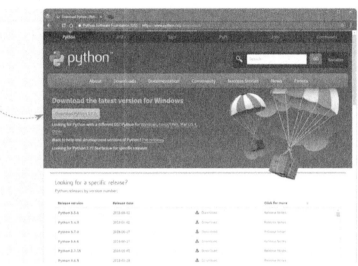

Step4. Once your download is complete, click on it to begin installation. There will be a pop up window.

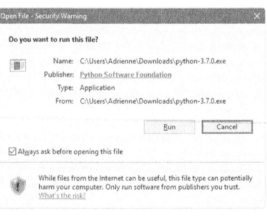

Step5. After download and installation, you can simply run the downloaded file, by double-clicking on the Python file. A dialog box will appear that looks like this:

Step6. Make sure the check the ADD PYTHON 3.7 TO PATH checkbox.

Step7. Then just click Install Now. Python will begin installation. A pop-up Window below will appear.

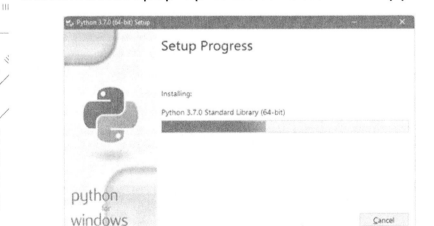

Step8. A few minutes later you should have a working Python installed on your system.

Step9. Yehey! You're done installing and you are ready to start your python journey on windows!

On Mac

Step1. On your computer, open an Internet browser like Google Chrome or Mozilla Firefox.

Step2. In the address bar, type "https://www.python.org/downloads/" to go to the official Python website's Downloads section.

Step3. Through the magic of coding, the website will probably know what type of computer you are using, and the DOWNLOAD button will show you the correct version of Python to install! In our case, we want the latest version, which was Python 3.7.0. Don't worry if it tells you to download a newer version. You can also find the installer for your specific machine in the Files section.

Step4. After clicking on the version, a download should start. Wait for it to finish before starting the installer.

Step5. When you start the installer, you should see a window like this one:

Step6. Click the CONTINUE button. You'll then be presented with some important information that you can choose to read or not.

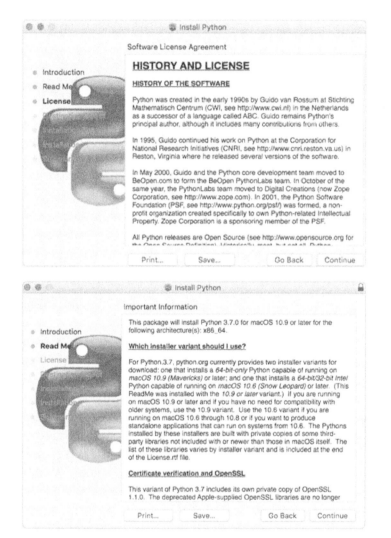

Step7. Click the CONTINUE button. Next you will see the license information.

Step8. Click the CONTINUE button. You'll be asked to agree to the terms of the software license agreement.

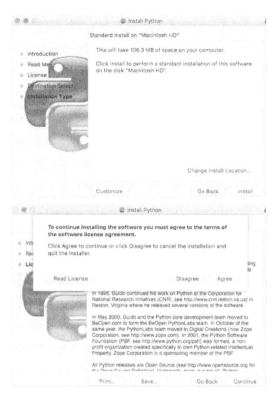

Step9. Click the AGREE button. You'll reach this final window:

Step10. Click the INSTALL button. If you need to, enter your personal user name and password for your account on your computer. Mac OS sometimes asks for this to make sure you want to install something. If you don't see this pop-up window, you can skip to the next step.

Step11. Installation should begin.

Step12. Wait for the installation to finish. Once it is done, you should see this:

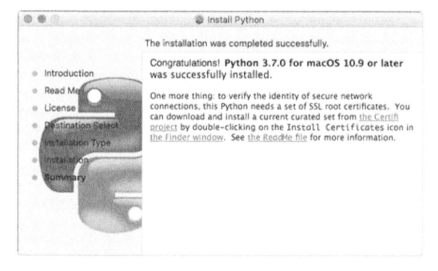

Step 14. Congratulate yourself! You've just installed Python on your Mac!

After Installation

How to Run Python

Before we start running our first Python program,

it is important that we understand how we can run python programs. Running or executing or deploying or firing a program simply means that we are making the computer process instructions/lines of codes. For instance, if the lines of codes (program) require the computer to display some message, then it should. The following are the ways or mode of running python programs. The interpreter is a special program that is installed when installing the Python package and helps convert text code into a language that the computer understands and can act on it (executing).

Immediate Mode

It is a way of running python programs that are not written in a file. We get into the immediate mode by typing the word python in the command line and which will trigger the interpreter to switch to immediate mode. The immediate mode allows typing of expressions directly, and pressing enter generates the output. The sign below is the Python prompt:

>>>

The python prompt instructs the interpreter to accept input from the user. For instance, typing 2+2 and pressing enter will display 4 as the output. In a way, this prompt can be used as a calculator. If you need to exit the immediate mode, type quit() or exit().

Now type 5 +3, and press enter, the output should be 8. The next mode is the Script Mode.

Script Mode

The script mode is used to run a python program written in a file; the file is called a script.

Integrated Development Environment (IDE)

An IDE provides a convenient way of writing and running Python programs. One can also use text editors to create a python script file instead of an IDE by writing lines of codes and saving the file with a .py extension. However, using an IDE can simplify the process of writing and running Python programs. The IDEL present in the Python package is an example of an IDE with a graphical user interface and gets installed along with the Python language. The advantages of IDE include helping getting rid of repetitive tasks and simplify coding for beginners. IDE provides syntax highlighting, code hinting, and syntax checking among other features. There also commercial IDE such as the PyScripter IDE that performs most of the mentioned functions.

Note

We have presented what Python is, how to download and install Python, the immediate and script modes of Python IDE, and what is an IDE.

Your First Program in Python

The rest of the illustrations will assume you are running the python programs in a Windows environment.

1. Start IDLE

2. Navigate to the File menu and click New Window

3. Type the following:

4. Print ("Hello World!")

5. On the file, menu click on Save. Type the name of myProgram1.py

6. Navigate to Run and click Run Module to run the program.

The first program that we have written is known as the "Hello World!" and is used to not only provide an introduction to a new computer coding language but also test the basic configuration of the IDE. The output of the program is "Hello World!" Here is what has happened, the Print() is an inbuilt function, it is prewritten and preloaded for you, is used to display whatever is contained in the () as long as it is between the double quotes. The computer will display anything written within the double quotes.

First Try!

Assignment

Now write and run the following python programs:

a) print("I am now a Python Language Coder!")

b) print("This is my second simple program!")

c) print("I love the simplicity of Python")

d) print("I will display whatever is here in quotes such as owyhen2589gdbnz082")

Now we need to write a program with numbers, but before writing such a program, we need to learn something about Variables and Types.

Remember python is object-oriented and it is not statically typed which means we do not need to declare variables before using them or specify their type. Let us explain this statement; an object-oriented language simply means that the language supports viewing and manipulating real-life scenarios as groups with subgroups that can be linked and shared mimicking the natural order and interaction of things. Not all programming languages are object-oriented; for instance, Visual C programming language is not object-oriented. In programming, declaring variables means that we explicitly state the nature of the variable. The variable can be declared as an integer, long integer, short integer, floating integer, a string, or as a character including if it is accessible locally or globally. A variable is a storage location that changes values depending on conditions.

For instance, number1 can take any number from 0 to infinity. However, if we specify explicitly that int number1 it then means that the storage location will only accept integers and not fractions for instance, fortunately or unfortunately, python does not require us to explicitly state the nature of the storage location (declare variables) as that is left to the python language itself to figure out that.

Before tackling types of variables and rules of writing variables, let us run a simple program to understand what variables when coding a python program are.

Start IDLE

Navigate to the File menu and click New Window

Type the following:

```
num1=4

num2=5

sum=num1+num2

print(sum)
```

On the file, menu click on Save. Type the name of myProgram2.py

Navigate to Run and click Run Module to run the program.

The expected output of this program should be "9" without the double quotes.

Explanation

At this point, you are eager to understand what has just happened and why the print(sum) does not have double quotes like the first programs we wrote. Here is the explanation.

The first line num1=4 means that variable num1(our shortened way of writing number1, first number) has been assigned 4 before the program runs.

The second line num2=5 means that variable

num2 (our shortened way of writing number2, second number) has been assigned 5 before the program runs.

The computer interprets these instructions and stores the numbers given

The third line sum=num1+num2 tells the computer that takes whatever num1 has been given and add to whatever num2 has been given. In other terms, sum the values of num1 and num2.

The fourth line print(sum) means that display whatever sum has. If we put double quotes to sum, the computer will display the word sum and not the sum of the two numbers! Remember that cliché that computers are garbage in and garbage out. They follow what you give them!

Note

+ is an operator for summing variables and has other users.

Now let us try out three Assignments involving numbers before we explain types of variables and rules of writing variables so that you get more freedom to play with variables. Remember variables values vary for instance num1 can take 3, 8, 1562, 1.

Follow the steps of opening the Python IDE and do the following:

The output should be 54

```
num1=43

num2=11

sum=num1+num2

print(sum)

The output should be 167

num1=101

num2=66

sum=num1+num2

print(sum)

The output should be 28

num1=9

num2=19

sum=num1+num2

print(sum)
```

CHAPTER - 2

WHERE TO START: THE BASICS

Variables

Variables are names for values. In Python the = symbol assigns the value on the right to the name on the left. The variable is created when a value is assigned to it. Here is a Python program that assigns an age to a variable age and a name in quotation marks to a variable first_name.

```
age = 42

first_name = 'Eunice'
```

Types of Variables

Now that we have defined what are variables are and the rules to write variable names, let us explore different types of variables.

A) Numbers

The Python accommodates two kinds of numbers, namely floating-point numbers and integer numbers. Python also supports complex numbers. When you sign a value to a number, then a number object is created. For example:

```
number3 =9

number4=12
```

Different Numerical Types Supported in Python

- long for example 681581903L

- int for example 11, 123, -151

- float for example 0.5, 23.1, -54.2

- complex for example 4.12j

Exercise

Identify the type of numerical below:

a. 234, 19, 312

b. 4.56, 2.9, 9.3

c. 7618925146829012762447

Identify the numerical type suitable for the following contexts:

d. Salary amount.

e. Counting the number of students in a class.

f. Getting the census figure in an entire country of China.

B) Strings

A sequence of characters. The character is just a symbol. For example, the English language contains 26 characters.

Computers do not deal with characters, but rather numbers (binary). Although you may see characters on your screen, it is internally stored and processed as a combination of 0 and 1.

Transforming a character into a cipher number is called, and the inverse process is decoding. ASCII and Unicode are some popular codecs used.

In Python, the string is a string of Unicode characters. Unicode was introduced to include every letter in all languages and bring uniformity into coding. You can learn more about Unicode here.

How to create a string in Python?

Strings can be created by enclosing characters within a single quotation mark or double quotation marks. Even triple quotes can be used in Python but are generally used to represent multi-line strings and lines.

all of the following are equivalent

```
my_string ='Hello'

print(my_string)

my_string ="Hello"

print(my_string)

my_string ='''Hello'''

print(my_string)
```

triple quotes string can extend multiple lines

```
my_string ="""Hello, welcome to

    the world of Python"""

print(my_string)
```

How To Use The Variables?

Now that you know how to assign variables to different values, the next step is understanding how to use them right. Let's create a scenario running from a previous one of calculating how much you'll have to save daily to be able to buy yourself a present at the end of the year. Imagine at the end of the year, you're unable to save the exact amount of money to buy yourself the dream gift, but your dad, seeing your efforts, asks you for the amount left so he can add up to it to get you your gift.

You only have to use your Python shell and assign variables to calculate it. Let's see...

```
Amount_needed= $40

Amount_in_hand=$33.75
```

Since regular math makes us understand that you'd have to subtract the amount you have from the amount needed to know how much will be left, then you have...

```
Amount_left=Amount_needed – Amount_in_hand
```

We have assigned our chosen variables to the values we have. All we have to do next is to input this into the Python shell and print the answer you're looking to get (i.e. print Amount_left) and see the outcome it gives. Just in case your saving goals are the same as mine, you should get $6.25. This means that your dad is going to give you $6.25 extra. Remember that while calculating with Python, you don't need to include the units (miles, sheets, dollars, or $) they stand for, just the numbers.

In the case that you get to the store, and you find out that your dream present has increased to $43, you can still use the same variable, only that you'll change it to contain the new value. Here's how you can input it in your Python shell. On a new line, enter Amount_needed= $43. Then, copy and paste the equation to calculate the answer again, to give you:

Amount_left=Amount_needed – Amount_in_hand

Then, go ahead to print your new answer.

Calculating With Python: Numbers And Operators

Python Numbers: Are they different from regular numbers?

Because you want to ask our program to solve the right equations (because computer language isn't 100% human language), you need to know the basic types of numbers that exist in the Python language. The first is the integers. They are the regular whole numbers that we use when counting, doing basic math, or telling our age like 0, 1, 89, 20225, and negatives like -88. The other is the floating-point numbers or floats for short, which are the decimal numbers like 0.8, 2.0, and 7.888 used to describe fractions.

Basic Python Operators

When you want to make mathematical calculations, the most common operations you perform are addition, subtraction, multiplication, and division, right? Those basic symbols we use to represent this operation are what we call operators in Python. The + (plus), - (minus), * (multiply by), and / (divide) represent the effect and calculations we want our set of numbers to have in that particular equation. So, if you input 3*4, you want to multiply your first number 3 by 4, which gives you 12.

Less Basic Python Operators

With Python, you can go further and perform mathematical calculations that your basic calculators don't provide for you. They are the exponent and modulus. As technical as they may sound, they are pretty straightforward operations. Not to worry, the only reason they are referred to as 'less basic' is because they are not the regular ones you're exposed to. Imagine you have to multiply a particular number by itself a number of times, say multiply 5 by itself 6 times. You do this using the exponent operator, which is the double asterisk (**). Now instead of typing 5*5*5*5*5*5, you only have to type 5**6 and get the same answer. It is the same as when you have 56 in a math problem.

In regular math, when you divide integers by other integers (remember integers?) and the numbers don't divide evenly, you have a remainder. In Python, going through the normal division route doesn't show you what remainder is left. You only get the whole number answer. For instance, 5/2 gives you 2 in Python. In the actual sense, there's a remainder of 1. To fix this, Python provides a special operator that allows you to check the remainder of your division equation. We call it modulus. It's represented by the percent (%) symbol. So, to get the remainder of 5/2, you input 5%2 and get 1.

Order of Operations

Now that you understand the basic and not so basic operators that can be used when calculating with Python, you should also know that there's a particular order that the operators have to follow to get correct answers and program right. There's only one way you can input your different operators in whichever order you wish to have them and still get the right answer. But before going into that exception, it's important that you're reminded about the order that the math rule (and Python in turn) follows. It is exponent first, then multiplication and division, then addition and subtraction. So, if you input 2 + 2 * 4 into a Python program, you'll be getting 10. If your intention is for the program to add up 2 and 2 before multiplying the answer by 4 and get 16, you'll have to go a little mile further.

Here's where the exception we spoke about a few words ago comes in. You have the option of adding parentheses or round brackets as they're regularly called. The parentheses indicate that you want the operation inside the brackets to go first before the others follow. So, in this case, when you input

(2+2)*4, you'll get 16 instead of the 10 when you carry out the operation without a round bracket. You can also have parentheses inside another parentheses. Say, ((5 + 10) * 20) / 10. With this, you're telling the computer to operate on the innermost bracket first, then go into the outer bracket, and then the rest of the equation according to the basic math rules. In this case, you get 30. This works because all the mathematical rules that you know apply to Python, and other programming languages.

CALCULATING IN THE PYTHON SHELL

You sure do know how to do regular calculations on pen and paper or on calculators. But how do you do math with Python? Here's how you go about it:

You start a Python shell by double-clicking the IDLE icon on your desktop. You get a >>> symbol which is the command prompt where you can input whatever it is you want your computer to process, which in this case is a math calculation. Try typing in a basic calculation like 7+6, and press ENTER. You should see the answer to your equation, which is 13.

You can also use the Python program to solve your daily mathematical problems, like knowing how much you'd need to save daily to achieve your goal of buying yourself a present at the end of the year. You can try this out on your own Python shell and see how much you should put into your piggy bank daily.

Comments

When writing python programs and indeed any programming language, comments are very important. Comments are used to describe what is happening within a program. It becomes easier for another person taking a look at a program to have an idea of what the program does by reading the comments in it. Comments are also useful to a programmer as one can forget the critical details of a program written. The hash (#) symbol is used before writing a comment in Python. The comment extends up to the newline character. The python interpreter normally ignores comments. Comments are meant for programmers to understand the program better.

Example

i.   Start IDLE

ii. Navigate to the File menu and click New Window

iii. Type the following:

```
#This is my first comment

#The program will print Hello World

Print('Hello World')   #This is an inbuilt function
to display
```

On the file, menu click on Save. Type the name of myProgram5.py

Navigate to Run and click Run Module to run the program

Assignment

This Assignment integrates most of what we have covered so far.

Write a program to sum two numbers 45, and 12 and include single line comments at each line of code.

Write a program to show the names of two employees where the first employee is "Daisy" and the second employee is "Richard." Include single comments at each line of code.

Write a program to display the student registration numbers where the student names and their registration are: Yvonne=235, Ian=782, James=1235, Juliet=568.

Multi-line Comments

Just like multi-line program statements we also have multi-line comments. There are several ways of writing multi-line comments. The first approach is to type the hash (#) at each comment line starting point.

For Example

Start IDLE.

Navigate to the File menu and click New Window.

Type the following:

```
#I am going to write a long comment line

#the comment will spill over to this line

#and finally end here.
```

The second way of writing multi-line comments involves using triple single or double quotes: ''' or ''. For multi-line strings and multi-line comments in Python, we use the triple quotes. Caution: When used in docstrings they will generate extra code, but we do not have to worry about this at this instance.

Example

Start IDLE.

Navigate to the File menu and click New Window.

Type the following:

```
"This is also a great

illustration of

a multi-line comment in Python."
```

CHAPTER - 3
THE MAGIC REIGN OF LISTS

What Is A List?

In your Python shell, you'll input it as favorite_colors= ['red', 'blue', 'purple', 'green']. You then ask your computer to print(favorite_colors), and you get all the items on your list as [red, blue, purple, green].

You may be wondering what the list and a string is. A list has a number of features that a string doesn't have. It allows you to add, remove, or pick one or some of the characters in the list. Imagine over the next few years, you decide you have one more favorite color you want to add to your existing list, or you no longer like a particular color, a list in Python allows you manipulate it.

A string can't allow you to add or remove without changing the entire characters in it. We could print the second item in the favorite_colors (blue) by entering its position in the list (called the index position) inside square brackets ([]). Index position is the position the computer sees the items in the list as. To computers, index positions begin from 0 (instead of the regular 1 we're all used to). So, the first item on your list is in index position 0, the second item is in index position 1, and so on.

You'll enter something like, print(favorite_colors[1]) in your Python shell. You'll get blue after hitting ENTER.

To change an item in your existing list, you'll enter it this way:

```
favorite_colors[1]= 'yellow'

print(favorite_colors)

You'll now have:

['red', 'yellow', 'purple', 'green'] as your list.
```

You have successfully removed the item 'blue' and replaced it with 'yellow' at index position 1.

You may also wish to show only some part of your list. You do this by using a colon (:) inside square brackets. For example, enter the following in your command prompt to see the second and third items on your list.

```
print(color_list[1:3])
```

Writing [1:3] is the same as saying, 'show the items from index position 1 up to (but not including) index position 3' – or in other words, items 2 and 3. This process is called slicing.

In this case, append adds an item to the end of a list. It goes this way:

```
color_list.append('white')

print(color_list)

['red', 'yellow', 'purple', 'green', 'white']
```

To remove items from a list, use the del command (short for delete). To remove the third item on your list, it's:

```
del color_list[2]

print(color_list)

['red', 'yellow', 'green', 'white']
```

We can also join lists by adding them, just like adding numbers, using a plus (+) sign.

If your first list includes numbers 1 to 3, and your second list includes random words, you can join them as one list. Here's how:

```
second_list=['buckle', 'my', 'shoes']

print(first_list + second_list)

After hitting ENTER, you get:

[1, 2, 3, 'buckle', 'my', 'shoes']
```

Working With Lists

Now, we have obtained one piece of information. Moving to the next one, let us find out what is at the start of this list. To do that, we will call up the first element, and this is where the concept of index position comes in.

An index is the position of a component. Here, the first component is 'Joey' and to find out that, we will do this:

```
friends = ["Joey", "Chandler", "Ross", "Phoebe", "Rachel", "Monica"]

print(friends[0])
```

Here, we will use the square brackets and use the value of zero. Why zero and not one? In Python, and in quite a few languages as well, the first position is always a zero. Here, "friends[0]" essentially tells the program to print the component with the first index position. The output, obviously, is:

Joey

Similarly, let's print the rest out accordingly!

```python
friends = ["Joey", "Chandler", "Ross", "Phoebe", "Rachel", "Monica"]

print(friends[0])

print(friends[1])

print(friends[2])

print(friends[3])

print(friends[4])

print(friends[5])
```

Output:

Joey

Chandler

Ross

Phoebe

Rachel

Monica

There is another way to do this. Suppose you do not know the length of the list, and you wish to print out the last recorded entry of the same, you can do that by using the following method:

```
friends = ["Joey", "Chandler", "Ross", "Phoebe",
"Rachel", "Monica"]

print(friends[-1])
```

Output:

Monica

The '-1' will always fetch you the last entry. If you use '-2' instead, it will print out the second to last entry as shown here:

```
friends = ["Joey", "Chandler", "Ross", "Phoebe",
"Rachel", "Monica"]

print(friends[-2])
```

Output:

Rachel

There are other variations involved here, as well. You can call the items from a specific starting point. Using the same list above, let's assume we wish the prompt to print out the last three entries only. We can do that easily by using the starting index number of the value we wish to print. In this case, it would be the index number '3':

```
friends = ["Joey", "Chandler", "Ross", "Phoebe", "Rachel", "Monica"]

print(friends[3:])
```

Output:

```
['Phoebe', 'Rachel', 'Monica']
```

You can also limit what you wish to see on the screen further by setting a range of index numbers. The first number, the one before the colon, represents the starting point. The number that you input after the colon is the endpoint. In our list of friends, we have a range from zero to five, let us narrow our results down a little:

```
friends = ["Joey", "Chandler", "Ross", "Phoebe", "Rachel", "Monica"]

print(friends[2:5])
```

Output:

```
['Ross', 'Phoebe', 'Rachel']
```

Remember, the last index number will not be printed; otherwise, the result would have also shown the last entry.

You can modify the values of a list quite easily. Suppose you wish to change the entry at index number five of the above list, and you wish to change the entry from 'Monica' to 'Geller,' this is how you would do so:

```
friends = ["Joey", "Chandler", "Ross", "Phoebe", "Rachel", "Monica"]

friends[5] = "Geller"

print(friends)
```

Output:

```
['Joey', 'Chandler', 'Ross', 'Phoebe', 'Rachel', 'Geller']
```

It is that easy! You can use lists with loops and conditional statements to iterate over random elements and use the ones which are most suitable to the situation. Practice a little, and you should soon get the hang of them.

What about if you wish to add numbers or values to the existing lists? Do we have to scroll all the way up and continue adding numbers manually? No! There are things called methods, which you can access at any given time to carry out various operations.

Here's a screengrab to show just how many options you have available to you once you press the '.' Key:

```
numbers = [99, 123, 2313, 1, 1231411, 343, 435345]
numbers.|
    insert(self, index, object)                          list
    append(self, object)                                 list
    clear(self)                                          list
    copy(self)                                           list
    count(self, object)                                  list
    extend(self, iterable)                               list
    index(self, object, start, stop)                     list
    pop(self, index)                                     list
    remove(self, object)                                 list
    reverse(self)                                        list
    sort(self, key, reverse)                             list
```

We will not be talking about all of these, but we will briefly look at some basic methods that every programmer should know.

Straight away, the 'append' method is what we use to add values. Simply type in the name of the list you wish to recall, followed by ".append" to let the program know you wish to add value. Type in the value, and that is it!

The problem with using the append method is that it adds the item randomly. What if you wish to add value to a specific index number? To do that, you will need to use the insert method.

Using an insert method, you will need to do this:

```
numbers = [99, 123, 2313, 1, 1231411, 343, 435345]

numbers.insert(2, 999)

print(numbers)
```

Output:

```
[99, 123, 999, 2313, 1, 1231411, 343, 435345]
```

The number was added right where I wanted. Remember to use an index position that is valid. If you are unsure, use the len() function to recall how many components are within a list. That should then allow you to know the index positions available.

You can also remove items from a list as well. Simply use the remove() method and input the number/value you wish to remove. Please note that if your list has more than one value that is exactly the same, this command will only remove the first instance only.

Let us assume you are presented with a list of mixed entries. There is no order that they follow. The numbers are just everywhere, disregarding the order. If you wish, you can sort the entire list to look more appealing by using the sort() method.

```
numbers = [99, 123, 2313, 1, 1231411, 99, 435345]

numbers.sort()

print(numbers)
```

Output:

```
[1, 99, 99, 123, 2313, 435345, 1231411]
```

You know, you can also have it the other way around by using the reverse() method. Try it!

To completely empty a list, you can use the clear() method. This specific method will not require you to pass any argument as a parameter. There are other methods such as pop() (which takes away the last item on the list only) that you should experiment with. Do not worry; it will not crash your system down or expose it to threats. The IDE is like a safe zone for programmers to test out various methods, programs, and scripts. Feel free and feel at ease when charting new waters.

Tuples

As funny as the name may be, tuples are pretty much like lists. The only major difference is that these are used when you do not wish for certain specialized values to change throughout the program. Once you create a tuple, it cannot be modified or changed later on.

Tuples are represented by parenthesis (). If you try and access the methods, you will no longer have access to the methods that you did when you were using lists. These are secure and used only in situations where you are certain you do not wish to change, modify, add, or remove items. Normally, we will be using lists, but it is great to know we have a safe way to do things as well.

Dictionaries

Unlike tuples and lists, dictionaries are different. To begin with, they work with "key-value pairs," which sounds confusing, I know. However, let us look at what exactly a dictionary is and how we can call, create, and modify the same.

To help us with the explanation, we have our imaginary friend here named James, who has graciously accepted to volunteer for the exercise. We then took some information from him such as his name, email, age, the car he drives, and we ended up with this information:

Name – James

Age – 58

Email – james@domain.com

Car – Tesla T1

What we have here are called key pairs. To represent the same within a dictionary, all we need is to create one. How do we do that? Let's have a look.

```
friend = {
"name": "James",
"age": 30,
"email": "james@domain.com",
"car": "Tesla T1"
}
```

We define a dictionary using {} braces. Add each pair as shown above with a colon in the middle. Use a comma to separate items from one another. Now, you have a dictionary called 'friend' and you can access the information easily.

Now, to call up the email, we will use square brackets as shown here:

```
friend = {

"name": "James",

"age": 30,

"email": "james@domain.com",

"car": "Tesla T1"

}

print(friend["email"])
```

Output:

james@domain.com

Similarly, try recalling the other elements to try it out yourself. Once again, I remind you that Python is case sensitive. If you recall 'age' as 'Age', it will not work at all.

Suppose you wish to recall an item without knowing the key pairs within a dictionary. If you type in a key named 'dob', the program is going to return an error like this:

Traceback (most recent call last):

```
    File "C:/Users/Programmer/PycharmProjects/
PFB/Lists2.py", line 7, in <module>

print(friend["dob"])

KeyError: 'dob'
```

There is a way you can check for values without the program screaming back at you with red/pink fonts. Use the .get() method instead, and the program will simply say 'None,' which represents the absence of value.

You can also give any keypair, that may not have existed before, a default value as well.

```
friend = {

"name": "James",

"age": 30,

"email": "james@domain.com",

"car": "Tesla T1"

}

print(friend.get("dob", "1, 1, 1900"))

Output:

1, 1, 1900
```

Unlike tuples, you can add, modify, or change values within a dictionary. I have already shown you how to do that with lists, but just for demonstration purposes, here's one way you can do that.

```
friend["age"] = 60

print(friend["age"])

Output:

60
```

CHAPTER - 4

FUN WITH LOOPS, LOOPS, LOOPS...

What Is A Loop?

WLoops are going to be another great topic that we are able to work with when it comes to Python. Loops are a good way to clean up some of the code that you want to work with so that you can make sure that enough shows up in your code, without having to write out as many lines. For example, if you have a code that you would like to work with that lists out the numbers gong one from fifty, you do not want to actually write out that many lines of code in the process. You can work with these loops instead to make sure that it is able to write out the lines, but it is really just a short amount of code. These loops are then able to hold onto a ton of information and will only use a few lines of code to make it happen.

There are a lot of things and a ton of data that we are then able to add into the loop, but you will find that these are actually pretty easy for us to work with anyway. These loops are going to be there to tell the compiler that it needs to continue reading through one or two lines of code over and over again until the conditions that you add into it are met.

So, if you are working on a program where you ask the compiler to write out numbers that go from one to ten, then the loop will tell your compiler to read through the numbers going from one to ten, then the loop will be set to go through the same line of code until it reaches ten. This can simplify the code while making sure that you are still able to get the things done that you would like.

When you work with all of these loops, it is important to remember to set up so that you have the condition in place before you ever try to work on the program. If you just go through and write out your loop, without adding in the condition that is needed, then the loop will start, but it will not know when to stop. The loop will just keep going through itself and will freeze the computer. Double-check before you run the program that the condition is in place before starting.

As you go through and create some of your own code with Python, there is going to be a few different loop types that you are able to work with. There are actually going to be many options, but we need to focus on the three main ones known as the while loop, the for loop, and the nested loop.

Using For Loops

The while loop can help us out with a lot of the different things that you want to accomplish when you are working on loops in this part of the code. In addition to handling some of the work with loops that the while loop can do, it is possible to work with them for a loop. When you are working with the for loops, you are working with the method that is considered the more traditional out of the two, and you can even make this the option that you use all of the time.

When you work with one of the for loops, your user will not go in and provide information to the code and then the loops start. Rather, with the for loop, Python is set up to go through an iteration in the order that it shows up on the screen. There is no need for input from the user because it just continues through the iteration until the end occurs. An example of a code that shows how a for loop works is the following:

Measure some strings:

```
words = ['apple', 'mango', 'banana', 'orange']

for w in words:

print(w, len(w))
```

Write this code into your compiler and then execute it. The for loop is going to make sure that all the words in the line above it are shown up on the screen, exactly how you wrote them out. If you want them in a different order, you need to do that as you work on the code, not later on. You can add in any words or other information that you want to show up in this kind of loop, just make sure that you have it in the right order from the beginning.

Using While Loop

The first type of loop that we are going to work on is the while loop. This loop is one that you can choose for your code when you know the specific number of times you want the code to cycle through that loop. You would use it to finish counting to ten for example. This one will need to have a condition, in the end, to make sure that it stops at the right point and doesn't keep going forever. It is also a good option if you want to ensure that your loop occurs at least one time before it moves on to the next part of the code. A good example of the while loop is the following code:

#calculation of simple interest. Ask the user to input the principal, rate of interest, number of years.

```
counter = 1

while(counter <= 3):

principal  =  int(input("Enter  the  principal
amount:"))

numberofyeras = int(input("Enter the number
of years:"))

rateofinterest = float(input("Enter the rate of
interest:"))

simpleinterest = principal * numberofyears *
rateofinterest/100

print("Simple interest = %.2f" %simpleinterest)

#increase the counter by 1

counter = counter + 1

print("You have calculated simple interest for 3
time!")
```

With the example that we did above, you will find that the user is able to place in the information that makes the most sense for them and the program. The code is then going to give them the interest rate based on the information that the user provides to it. For this one, we are going to set up the while at the beginning of the code and then told it to only go through the loop a maximum of three times. You will then be able to change up the code as well to make sure that it will go through the loops as many times as you would like.

Nested Structures

We can also finish this out with a look at how the nested loop is going to work. This is a more advanced type of loop that is going to combine two of the other loop types together in order to get them to run at the same time. There are a number of instances where you can work with this nested loop, and it is often going to depend on the kind of code that you would like to complete and what you are hoping to get out of it.

The third type of loop that we are able to work with here is going to be known as the nested loop. Any time that you are working with this loop, you are basically going to take one of the other types of loops and then you will place it inside of a different loop. Both of these loops will end up running in the code at the same time, and they will both continue on until they are complete. There are a number of situations where you will want to focus on these nested loops to help you finish your code.

For example, you may find that you would like to work on a nested loop that can create a new multiplication table, the nested loop is going to be a good one to get it done. The code that we need to use in order to make this one work for our needs and to see how a nested loop is going to work will include:

#write a multiplication table from 1 to 10

```
For x in xrange(1, 11):

For y in xrange(1, 11):

Print '%d = %d' % (x, y, x*x)
```

When you got the output of this program, it is going to look similar to this:

```
1*1 = 1

1*2 = 2

1*3 = 3

1*4 = 4
```

All the way up to 1*10 = 2

Then it would move on to do the table by twos such as this:

```
2*1 =2

2*2 = 4
```

And so on until you end up with 10*10 = 100 as your final spot in the sequence

Any time you need to get one loop to run inside another loop, the nested loop will be able to help you get this done. You can combine together the for loop, the while loop, or each combination based on what you want to get done inside the code. But it definitely shows you how much time and space inside the code that these loops can save. The multiplication table above only took up four lines to write out and you got a huge table. Think of how long this would take if you had to write out each part of the table!

The for loop, the while loop, and the nested loop are going to be some of the most common loops that a beginner is able to focus on when it is time to write out their own codes in this language. You are able to use these codes to make sure that you can get a ton done in some of the programs that you have chosen, without having to focus as much on writing out a ton of lines. You are even able to do this in a manner that will make sure that certain parts of the code will read through themselves again, without you having to rewrite it at all. There are many times when you will want to handle writing loops in your code, and learning how to make each one work can help make your code stronger.

Errors

Syntax Error

When a Python interpreter encounters an error in the program, it terminates the program and displays an error message to the user. Syntax represents the structure of a program and the rules of declaring that structure. If there is a single error, Python will quit and you will not be able to run the program.

If you're new to programming, you may spend a few days tracking syntax errors. Once you become familiar with the language, however, you will make fewer errors, and it will be easy to track them.

Runtime Error

A runtime errors occurs after running the program. That is, the error will not show up until you run the program. Runtime errors are commonly known as exceptions as they indicate something has already happened.

Semantic Errors

If a program has a semantic error, the program will run successfully and the Python interpreter will not generate the error message. The program will run up to the end but will not perform the task it was meant to do.

To correct semantic errors, you have to look at the program output and work backwards by analyzing what each output was supposed to do.

CHAPTER - 5

BETTER THE QUESTION BETTER THE ANSWER: IF STATEMENT

Comparison operators are special operators in Python programming language that evaluate to either True or False state of the condition. Program flow control refers to a way in which a programmer explicitly species the order of execution of program code lines. Normally, flow control involves placing some condition (s) on the program code lines. The most basic form of these conditional statements is the if statement. This one is going to provide us with some problems right from the beginning. But knowing a bit about it will help us to get the if else and other control statements to work the way that we want.

To start, the if statement is going to take the input of the user, and compare it to the condition that you set. If the condition is met here, then the code will continue on, usually showing some kind of message that you set up in the code.

However, if the input does not match up with the condition that you set the returned value will be False.

The If structures

This is the simplest decision structure. It includes a statement or block of statements on the "True" path only.

The general form of the Python statement is

if Boolean_Expression:

\# Here goes

\# a statement or block of statements

In the next example, the message "You are underage!" displays only when the user enters a value less than 18. Nothing is displayed when the user enters a value that is greater than or equal to 18.

```
file_13 _1 a

age = int(input( "Enter your age: " ))

if age < 18:

print( "You are underage!" )
```

The If-Then-Else Structure

The "if...else" statement will execute the body of if in the case that the tests condition is True. Should the if...else tests expression evaluate to false, the body of the else will be executed. Program blocks are denoted by indentation. The if...else provides more maneuverability when placing conditions on the code. The if...else syntax

if test condition:

Statements

else:

Statements

A program that checks whether a number is positive or negative

Start IDLE.

Navigate to the File menu and click New Window.

Type the following:

```
number_mine=-56
if(number_mine<0):
print(number_mine, "The number is negative")
else:
print(number_mine, "The number is a positive number")
```

Assignment

Write a Python program that uses if..else statement to perform the following

1. Given number=9, write a program that tests and displays whether the number is even or odd.

2. Given marks=76, write a program that tests and displays whether the marks arc above pass mark or not bearing in mind that pass mark is 50.

3. Given number=78, write a program that tests and displays whether the number is even or odd.

4. Given marks=27, write a program that tests and displays whether the marks are above pass mark or not bearing in mind that pass mark is 50.

Assignment

Write a program that accepts age input from the user, explicitly coverts the age into integer data types, then uses if...else flow control to tests whether the person is underage or not, the legal age is 21. Include comments and indentation to improve the readability of the program.

Other follow up work: Write programs in Python using if statement only to perform the following:

1. Given number=7, write a program to test and display only even numbers.

2. Given number1=8, number2=13, write a program to only display if the sum is less than 10.

3. Given count_int=57, write a program that tests if the count is more than 45 and displays, the count is above the recommended number.

4. Given marks=34, write a program that tests if the marks are less than 50 and display the message, the score is below average.

5. Given marks=78, write a program that tests if the marks are more than 50 and display the message, great performance.

6. Given number=88, write a program that tests if the number is an odd number and displays the message, Yes it is an odd number.

7. Given number=24, write a program that tests and displays if the number is even.

8. Given number =21, write a program that tests if the number is odd and displays the string, Yes it is an odd number.

The If-elif structure

Now think of scenarios where we need to evaluate multiple conditions, not just one, not just two but three and more. Think of where you have to choose team member, if not Richard, then Mercy, if not Richard and Mercy then Brian, if not Richard, Mercy, and Brian then Yvonne. Real-life scenarios may involve several choices/conditions that have to be captured when writing a program.

Remember that the elif simply refers to else if

and is intended to allow for checking of multiple expressions. The if the block is evaluated first, then elif block(s), before the else block. In this case, the else block is more of a fallback option when all other conditions return false. Important to remember, despite several blocks available in if..elif..else only one block will be executed.. if...elif..else Syntax:

if test expression:

Body of if

elif test expression:

Body of elif

else:

Body of else

Example

Three conditions covered but the only one can execute at a given instance.

Start IDLE.

Navigate to the File menu and click New Window.

Type the following:

```
nNum= 1

if nNum == 0:

print("Number is zero.")
```

```
elif nNum > 0:

print("Number is a positive.")

else:

print("Number is a negative.")
```

Incidental using the If Statement

There are many things that you can do with values and variables, but the ability to compare them is something that will make it much easier for you to try and use Python. It is something that people will be able to do no matter what type of values that they have, and they can make sure that they are doing it in the right way so that their program will appear to be as smooth-running as possible.

To compare your variables is one of the many options that Python offers you, and the best way to do it is through an "if statement."

Now, you can create a new file. This is what you will need to be able to do. Do not forget indentation!

Here is the way that an incidental will look:

```
apples=6

bus = "yellow"
```

```
if apples == 0:

print ("Where are the apples?" )

else:

print ("Did you know that busses are %s?", bus)
```

Run the code through your python program. It will look like this.

```
Did you know that busses are yellow?
```

The easiest way to understand why the output looked like this is because the apples were not included with the variation. There were not zero apples, and that was something that created a problem with the code. For that reason, it wasn't put in the output because there was no way to do it and no way to make it look again.

To make sure that you are going to be able to use it with a not statement, you can use another if statement in combination with that not.

if not apples == 0

Now, you can try to run the code again through the program that you created.

Did you know that busses are yellow?

Both of the things that you wrote in the code are included with the statements, and then, you will be able to try different things. If you do not want to write out the not statement, you can simply use the "!"

```
apples=5

if apples!= 0:

    print("How about apples!")
```

When there is an input in your program, such as the number of apples that someone wants or a fact that they have that they can teach you about, the output will look the same. Either they will get a statement about the apples, or they will get a statement about the bus being yellow. If there are no apples that are put into the equation, then you will have the output show up as "Where are the apples"

The conditionals that you use are made up of simple expressions. When you break them down into even smaller pieces, it is easy to understand how they can be used and what you will be able to do with the expressions that you have in the things that you do. It will also give you the chance to be able to show that there is so much more than what you initially had with the variables and values.

Nested if Statements in Python

Sometimes it happens that a condition exists but there are more sub-conditions that need to be covered and this leads to a concept known as nesting. The amount of statements to nests is not limited but you should exercise caution as you will realize nesting can lead to user errors when writing code. Nesting can also complicate maintaining of code. The only indentation can help determine the level of nesting.

Example

Start IDLE.

Navigate to the File menu and click New Window.

Type the following:

```
my_charact=str(input("Type a character here either 'a', 'b' or 'c':"))

if (my_charact='a'):

if(my_charact='a'):

print("a")

else if:

(my_charact='b')

print("b")
```

```
else:

    print("c")
```

Assignment

Write a program that uses the if..else flow control statement to check non-leap year and display either scenario. Include comments and indentation to enhance the readability of the program.

Absolutes

There is a way to create the conditionals so that there is a block of codes that will show you whether or not there is a conditional, and it has something that it can do even if the conditional is not true and cannot be verified with the different things that you do.

That is where the absolute conditionals come into play.

You will need to see whether or not there are different things that you can put in.

Create the variable

apples

Now, you will need to put the input in with the different things that you have created a version of the file that you saved.

```
print "What is your age?"

age = input()
```

That is the way that you will be able to see how old someone is. But, how exactly does that relate to the number of apples you have?

It doesn't, it just shows you how the variable works so that people can put things in.

You'll create

```
apples = input ("What number of apples are there?/n")
```

That is the easiest part of it and will help you to create the variable that you need for the rest of it.

```
if apples == 1:

print ("I don't know what to do with just one apple!")
```

You'll get an error though because applesis actually just a string and you need to make it an integer.

Simple:

```
int(string)
```

Now it will look like this:

```
apples = input("What number of apples are
there?/n")

apples = int(apples)

if apples == 1:

print ("I don't know what to do with just one
apple!")
```

Put this whole string into your file or change the wording around a bit so that you can figure out what you want to do with it (that is truly great practice for you). When you have put it in, run it through.

The code will work because you created a variable, you added different elements to it, and you allowed for the input of the "apples" in the sequence so that you would be able to show how things worked with it.

This was one of the greatest ways that you could do new things, and it also allowed you the chance to be able to try new things so that you were doing more with it. While you are creating strings of integers, you will need to make sure that you are transforming them into integers instead of simple strings so that you can make sure that they show up and there are no error codes.

CHAPTER - 6

THE TURTLE GRAPHICS OF
YOUR DREAMS

What is Turtle

Turtle is a very handy Python tool. It is a module —we shall discuss what a module later— that helps us draw in Python.

Before we can use the turtle module, we need to import it. To import a module into Python, we use import <module name>

```
>>> import turtle
>>>
```

It looks like nothing happened; this is a good thing since we did not get an error. For example, if you try to import a module that does not exist, Python will return an error as shown below:

```
>>> import unknown_module
Traceback (most recent call last):
  File "<pyshell#2>", line 1, in <module>
    import unknown_module
ModuleNotFoundError: No module named 'unknown_module'
```

Now that we have imported Turtle, let us learn how to start using the turtle module. The first step is to create a drawing canvas where we shall do all our drawing. To create a canvas, simply use the pen() function.

```
>>> t = turtle.pen()
```

This will display a blank window with an arrow at the center. This window is what we call a canvas:

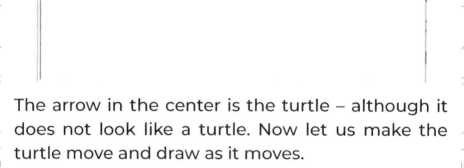

The arrow in the center is the turtle – although it does not look like a turtle. Now let us make the turtle move and draw as it moves.

The basic movements for the python turtle are; move forward, move backwards, turn left and turn right by various degrees. Let us make our turtle to move forward. We can do this by calling t.turtle() function. For example:

```
>>> t = turtle.Pen()
>>> t.forward(50)
```

From the above command, we tell Python to make t, which in this case refers to the turtle, to move forward by 50 pixels or by 50 points. In a computer, a pixel is the smallest point on the computer screen –your computer screen consists of very tiny dots called as pixels. This is an example of a highly magnified number on a computer screen.

So the python turtle moves forward while drawing. Let us make it go to the left using t.left() function.

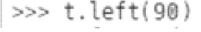

```
>>> t.left(90)
```

This tells the turtle to move left by 90 degrees. Now, if we want the turtle to turn right, we just change it to right(90). The diagram below shows which directions the turtle will take after angle variations.

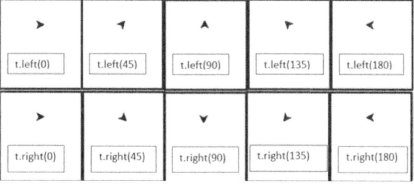

➤	◤	▲	➤	◀
t.left(0)	t.left(45)	t.left(90)	t.left(135)	t.left(180)
➤	◣	▼	▶	◀
t.right(0)	t.right(45)	t.right(90)	t.right(135)	t.right(180)

This time, let us make the turtle move 50 pixels forward in the left direction. For example:

This time, the turtle moves 50 pixels left to the left. Try completing the diagram by making a square. Did you manage to create the square – let us see how to create it.

```
>>> import turtle
>>> t = turtle.Pen()
>>> t.forward(50)
>>> t.left(90)
>>> t.forward(50)
>>> t.left(90)
>>> t.forward(50)
>>> t.left(90)
>>> t.forward(50)
```

Let us learn some more. Let us try a new function to see what happens.

```
>>> t.reset()
>>> |
```

Now, look at the turtle graphic – Where did our Square go?

We use the turtle reset() function to tell Python to delete everything created by the turtle module – quite damaging if you use it wrongly. You can also see that the turtle arrow returned to the default location. The reset function differs from the clear() function that does the same operation leaving the turtle at the current position. Let us see an illustration:

```
>>> t.clear()
>>>
```

What if we wanted our turtle to do a moonwalk, which is moving backwards while drawing? To get the python turtle to move backwards, we use the backward function(). For example:

```
>>> t.backward(200)
>>>
```

What if we wanted the turtle to go up or down without making any drawings. What would we do then? First, reset your turtle using the reset function. To make the turtle move up without drawing, we can use the up() function. The up() function makes the turtle move upwards by 30 pixels.

To make the turtle go down without drawing, we use the down() function. This also makes the turtle go down by 30 pixels. If you want to hide the turtle so that you can see what you have created, you can use the hideturtle() function.

Diagrams with straight lines are not the only thing you can create using turtle. To create a circle, we use the circle() function while entering the radius of the circle –the operation of entering values in a function is called parameter passing.

Here is how we create a circle – reset the turtle first before creating a circle:

```
>>> import turtle
>>> t = turtle.Pen()
>>> t.circle(60)
```

This time, look at the following lines of code and try to guess what they do. If you get them right, Pizza is on me

```
>>> t.reset()
>>> t.color("Green")
>>> t.circle(100)
>>> t.hideturtle()
```

Let us find out what the above lines of code actually do. The first line resets the turtle, the second line sets the color of the turtle to Green, the third creates a circle with a radius of 100, and the third line hides the turtle – I know I owe you a pizza▢.

We change the color of the turtle by simply using the color() function and passing the name of the color we want as the parameter.

We can also fill the drawing we created using the begin_tfill() and end_fill() functions. Let us fill our circle with the color Green.

```
>>> t.begin_fill()
>>> t.circle(100)
>>> t.end_fill()
```

We do not need to pass the color green in the begin_fill() function as we are already using color green – but in case we want another color, we have to enter the color.

NOTE: You MUST end the fill for the filling to be completed. Again, the filling works only if you close your drawing to prevent the color of the drawing from leaking out in the canvas.

Exercise

Try out the following exercise:

Question 1

Draw a red rectangle of length 40 pixels and 80 pixels. You should first import the turtle module, create canvas named my_pen, then draw the rectangle, and finally hide the turtle.

Question 2

Write a python program that creates three circles one inside the other. The first circle should have a radius of 60 pixels, the second one should have a radius of 40 pixels, and the last one a radius of 30 pixels. Each circle should have a different color fill from the others.

Question 3

Write a program that creates box that does not have corners as shown below:

Solutions

Let us look at sample solutions for the above questions – you can solve them in any way you find appropriate.

Solution 1

```
>>> import turtle
>>> my_pen = turtle.Pen()
>>> my_pen.color("Red")
>>> my_pen.forward(80)
>>> my_pen.left(90)
>>> my_pen.forward(40)
>>> my_pen.left(90)
>>> my_pen.forward(80)
>>> my_pen.left(90)
>>> my_pen.forward(40)
>>> my_pen.hideturtle()
```

Solution 2

```
>>> import turtle
>>> C = turtle.Pen()
>>> C.fillcolor("blue")
>>> C.begin_fill()
>>> C.circle(60)
>>> C.end_fill()
>>> C.fillcolor("yellow")
>>> C.begin_fill()
>>> C.Circle(40)
Traceback (most recent call last):
  File "<pyshell#8>", line 1, in <module>
    C.Circle(40)
AttributeError: 'Turtle' object has no attribute 'Circle'
>>> C.circle(40)
>>> C.end_fill()
>>> C.fillcolor("red")
>>> C.begin_fill()
>>> C.circle(30)
>>> C.end_fill()
>>> C.hideturtle()
```

Solution 3

```
>>> import turtle
>>> box = turtle.Pen()
>>> box.up()
>>> box.forward(10)
>>> box.down()
>>> box.forward(50)
>>> box.up()
>>> box.forward(10)
>>> box.left(90)
>>> box.forward(10)
>>> box.down()
>>> box.forward(50)
>>> box.up()
>>> box.forward(10)
>>> box.left(90)
>>> box.forward(10)
>>> box.down()
>>> box.forward(50)
>>> box.up()
>>> box.forward(10)
>>> box.left(90)
>>> box.forward(10)
>>> box.down()
>>> box.forward(50)
>>> box.hideturtle()
```

Were you able to work through these exercises on your own? If you did, you are doing amazingly well and are on your way to becoming a Python programming master.

CHAPTER - 7
WORKING WITH PYTHON FUNCTIONS

In this section, we are going to learn a very important programming technique known as Reduce, Reuse, and Recycle that falls under the category of functions in programming.

Loops are very effective if we are repeating an action many times over. However, if we want to repeat lines of code, we must use functions. A function is a block of code that contains other code within it to perform a task. We have used functions before.

In the background, without functions, we would have to enter a code like this every time we need to print out something on the screen:

```python
import collections as _collections
import re
import sys as _sys
import types as _types
from io import StringIO as _StringIO

__all__ = ["pprint","pformat","isreadable","isrecursive","saferepr",
           "PrettyPrinter"]


def pprint(object, stream=None, indent=1, width=80, depth=None, *,
           compact=False):
    """Pretty-print a Python object to a stream [default is sys.stdout]."""
    printer = PrettyPrinter(
        stream=stream, indent=indent, width=width, depth=depth,
        compact=compact)
    printer.pprint(object)

def pformat(object, indent=1, width=80, depth=None, *, compact=False):
    """Format a Python object into a pretty-printed representation."""
    return PrettyPrinter(indent=indent, width=width, depth=depth,
                         compact=compact).pformat(object)

def saferepr(object):
    """Version of repr() which can handle recursive data structures."""
    return _safe_repr(object, {}, None, 0)[0]

def isreadable(object):
    """Determine if saferepr(object) is readable by eval()."""
    return _safe_repr(object, {}, None, 0)[1]

def isrecursive(object):
    """Determine if object requires a recursive representation."""
    return _safe_repr(object, {}, None, 0)[2]

class _safe_key:
    """Helper function for key functions when sorting unorderable objects.

    The wrapped-object will fallback to a Py2.x style comparison for
    unorderable types (sorting first comparing the type name and then by
    the obj ids).  Does not work recursively, so dict.items() must have
    _safe_key applied to both the key and the value.

    """

    __slots__ = ['obj']

    def __init__(self, obj):
```

Once we create a function, we can then use it to perform the specified task whenever needed. Let us look at an example.

If you wanted to create a code for a rectangle and then create 10 other rectangles, you would have to type the code 10 times. The aspect of repeating code is not a fun part of programming.

For the rectangle problem, we can create a function that contains the code for creating the desired rectangle. We can then call the function to create the rectangle as many times as we want.

Example of functions that we already used include: print(), list(), range() —that is why they were using parenthesis. However, the functions we used were built-in functions, meaning they come preinstalled in Python. We can also create our own functions to reuse.

To create a function, we must understand its syntax. A python function has three key components. They include:

- a name

- function parameters

- function body

These three components work together as follows:

```
def function_name(parameters):

function_body
```

The function structure is similar to the structure of the for and while loops. You must indent the function body. The function name can be any name you like as long it follows the rules on naming a variable.

The next part is the parameters. Parameters are the variables that the function will be taking to perform its specific task. For example, in the print function, we passed either the number, a string, or a variable to print out. Parameters are not always required and you can create a function without parameters.

The function body contains the lines of code that define what the function does. For example, if you have a program that tests the maximum and minimum value between two numbers, you will write the code to test out this problem inside the function body.

Whenever you need to use a function, you just call the function using its name. If the function requires parameters, you MUST pass these parameters during the function call. Let us see an example that prints out the "Hello, I am your first function"

```
def print_me():
    print("I am your first function")
print_me()
```

Note that this is a function without parameters and thus, we did not need to pass them during the function call. Now we can use this function whenever we need it in the entire program.

Here are some of the reasons why functions are important:

- Simplifies the process of coding

- Allows for code reuse

- It makes debugging a lot easier –debugging is the process of finding and fixing errors in a program

- It reduces the code size and makes it clean and readable

Let us now see how to work with a function that has parameters. Use the max and min functions.

```
>>> def min_max(number1, number2):
        if (number1 > number2):
            print("Max number is %s"%number1)
        else:
            print("Maximum number is %s"%number2)
```

```
>>> min_max(10,20)
Maximum number is 20
```

Above, we declared a function called min_max that takes two arguments: number1 and number2. The function checks if the first number is greater than the second number. If it is, the maximum number is the first number; otherwise, the maximum number is the second number. During the function call, we passed in the numbers we wanted to test —in this case 10 and 20. The program then checks for the maximum and returns the value.

If you want to create a function that you can use across all your python programs, we create a file that contains the function code and then import it in other files.

Can you remember the toy business project we worked on earlier? We can create a python function to calculate the amount earned in one day. The parameters required are total number of toys, toys spoilt, and the cost of each toy. Create a new file and save it, making sure you remember the name of the file as well as the function name.

```python
def income_per_day(total_toys, toys_spoilt, cost_per_toy):
    total_money = (total_toys - toys_spoilt) * cost
    print("Total income = %S" %total_money)
```

To use the function in another file, simply create a new file and use the import module.

```python
from daily_income import income_per_day
cost_per_toy = 25
day1_total = input("Enter the total number of toys in that day: ")
day1_total = int(day1_total)
day1_spoilt = input("How many toys were spoilt: ")
day1_spoilt = int(day1_spoilt)
print("Day 1 result: ")

# function call
income_per_day(day1_total, day1_spoilt, cost_per_toy)
```

```
Enter the total number of toys in that day: 200
How many toys were spoilt: 10
Day 1 result:
Total income = 4750
```

Now we can use the income_per_day function in all the required programs. All we have to do is change the required arguments.

Variables created within a function are only visible within a function. For example, if you try to use the variable such as total_money in the main program, it will result in an error. This aspect of variable accessibility is what we refer to as a variable or function scope. Therefore, the variable such as total_money has a scope of its created function. This means that once the function executes, the attendant results is the immediate destruction of the variable.

If you want to use the result of a function call, we use the keyword return followed by the value we want returned. When Python comes across the return keyword in a function, it knows that it has come to the end of the function and returns the current value from the function call. However, you can only return one value from a function. The return keyword also indicates the end of the function execution and any code beyond the return keyword will not execute.

Let us test out your understanding of the various principles learned in this part of this python guidebook:

Exercise

Question 1

Write a python function that asks the user for a name input and the number of times to print the name. Use loops to solve this problem.

Question 2

Expand the toy business program we worked with earlier to calculate the income for five consecutive days —use loops.

Question 3

Write a python program that creates a rectangle using the python turtle module. Use the rectangle function to draw a bookshelf.

Now that we have had tons of practice writing python code and programs, we need to look at another important feature, a feature that you must master before you can master programming —in Python and in other programming languages:

Solution 1

```
def name(name, times):
    name = input("Enter your name: ")
    times = input("Enter the number of times: ")
    times = int(times)
    for in range(0, times):
        print(name)
name()
```

Solution 3

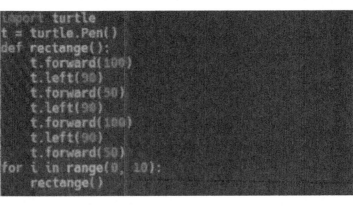

```
import turtle
t = turtle.Pen()
def rectange():
    t.forward(100)
    t.left(90)
    t.forward(50)
    t.left(90)
    t.forward(100)
    t.left(90)
    t.forward(50)
for i in range(0, 10):
    rectange()
```

Creating Your Own Functions

Let's learn how to create our own functions and make use of them within other scripts and programs. In order to tell Python that you would like to create a function, you can use the def keyword. The def keyword tells Python you want to define a function and that it needs to recognize a variety of keywords and values to follow. After using the def keyword, you need to provide the function name and any arguments/parameters your function will make use of. You can then begin writing the commands you'd like your function to carry out. In other words, the syntax for creating a function looks something like this:

```
def name(parameters):

Code to carry out desired actions
```

Your functions will often require another keyword, the return keyword. The return keyword specifies an expression, variable, or value you'd like the function to pass back out to the main program once the function has finished running. Once the return statement is executed, the function will stop running, and the expression you've designated will be passed back. Here's how to return an expression or value:

```
def name(parameters):

    Code to carry out desired actions

    return desiredExpression
```

If your function returns a value, you can assign that value to a variable by calling the function and assigning it to a variable. You can then manipulate the return value that has been stored in the variable.

returned_value = function_used(list of parameters)

If your function does not need to return a value, you can either just not use the return keyword or use return None.

Here's an example of a function that you can run in PyCharm:

```
def multiply_values(num_1, num_2):

    num_3 = 2

    print("Number 1 is : " + str(num_1))

    print("Number 2 is : " + str(num_2))

print("Number 3 is: " + str(num_3))

    mult_num = num_1 * num_2 * num_3
```

```python
        print("Product of multiplication is: " +
str(mult_num))

    return mult_num
```

The function takes in two different numbers as parameters, multiplies these numbers together, and then multiplies the product of those numbers by two. The function then returns the multiplied value. The function also prints out the numerical values that have been passed in, as well as the product of the multiplication.

We can now call the function, assign it to a variable, and then print the variable to make sure that the returned value is what we expect it to be.

```python
multiplied = multiply_values(8, 9)

print(multiplied)
```

You may notice that we have called the print function within our own function. Python allows you to call functions within functions like this, even your own custom functions.

CHAPTER - 8

PYTHON'S BUILT-IN FUNCTIONS

By now, you've seen that using functions can save you a huge amount of time and energy. Therefore, it will pay off to know about some commonly used Python functions. The functions listed below are all built-in to Python and can be called simply by invoking them with no imports needed. Also included in this section are methods, which act like functions, but only work on specific data types and structures. The methods are typically invoked using dot notation on the target object.

print() - We've already covered this extensively, but it prints out the provided arguments to your terminal or screen.

abs() - This returns the absolute value of the provided argument, assuming the value is a numerical value (a float or integer).

round() - Rounds the provided numerical value to the nearest integer.

min() - Finds and returns the smallest value in a list of values. It even works on strings, where it will select the earliest alphabetical characters.

max() - The opposite of min, finds the largest or alphabetically last values.

sorted() - Sorts a list in ascending order and works on both numerical values and strings.

sum() - Adds the elements of a list together and returns the sum.

len() - Counts and returns the number of elements in a list. If called on a string, it will return the number of characters in the string.

type() - Returns the data type of the variable that the function has been provided.

String Methods

lower() - Converts all elements of the string to lowercase.

upper() - Converts all elements of the string to uppercase.

strip() - Removes extra whitespace from the beginning or end of the string.

replace() - Takes two arguments and replaces the first string with the second string.

split() - Takes in a specified delimiter as an argument and splits the string on that delimiter (splits strings into a list, splitting whenever the specified character occurs).

join() - Joins elements of a list into a single string, and you can choose the delimiter to join on.

List Methods

append() - Adds the provided argument to a list.

remove() - Removes the provided argument from a list.

count() - Returns the index number of the given value in a list.

clear() - Removes all elements from a list.

Dictionary Methods

keys() - Gives all the keys found in the dictionary.

values() - Gives all the values found in the dictionary.

clear() - Deletes everything from the dictionary.

Functions and Imports Exercise

Functions are an incredibly important part of programming in Python, so let's be sure that we understand. We'll try another programming exercise, and this time, we will focus on functions and imports.

Try doing the following:

- Write a function that takes arguments and manipulates the values of those arguments in some way (bonus points for making use of *args or **kwargs). Return the results of the manipulation. Use local variables in the function.

- Save the file your function is in within your current folder.

- Create a new file.

- Import the function from your original file.

- Create some global variables and pass them into the function.

- Print the resulting value of the function.

After you've attempted this by yourself, you can review the example below to see one way of meeting the requirements for this exercise.

Here's one potential solution:

save this in a file called "shopping_list.py"

```
def shopping_list(store, *args):

    shopping_list = []

    for i in args:

        print("Adding {} to list".format(i))
```

```
    shopping_list.append(str(store) + " - " + str(i))

    return shopping_list
```

In another file in the same directory:

create a new file in the same directory (or alias the import)

```
from shopping_list import shopping_list as SL

grocery_list = SL("Hilltop Grocery", "bread", "milk", "coffee", "apple juice")

computer_list = SL("Top Computer Parts", "RAM", "keyboard", "USB hub")

print(grocery_list)

print(computer_list)
```

CHAPTER - 9
RESOURCES: USEFUL MODULES

Modules

Let's look at how to use some of Python's built-in functions. We've already gone over some of Python's included functions, like the print() function. These functions are part of the standard Python package. In contrast, some additional functions come with a Python installation but aren't available for use until you import them. Such functions are referred to as "modules."

In order to import a module, you can use one of several different import methods. The entire module can be imported by simply typing:

```
import name_of_module
```

For example, Python comes with a module called random, which can be used to generate random numbers. To import this module, you would just type:

```
import random
```

When you import a module with the above method, in order to use a function that the module possesses, you need to call the function using dot notation. For example, in order to make use of the randrange() function, you can use the following syntax:

```
random_nums = random.randrange(0, 25)
```

You can also assign shorthand or nicknames to a module that you import so that you don't have to write out the name of the module each time. For instance, we can alias random like this:

```
import random as r
```

We can now call the randrange function simply by writing:

```
random_nums2 = r.randrange(0, 25)
```

We can also import specific functions rather than importing an entire module. We can import specific functions by specifying the name of the module with from and then using the import keyword with the name of the functions we want to import.

from random import randrange

Importing a specific function this way enables us to just refer to the function by name when we want to use it:

```
random_nums3 = randrange(0, 25)
```

You can import multiple functions from a module by separating the name of the functions you wish to import with a comma. In general, if you don't need to use many functions from the module, it's a good idea to import just the functions you need rather than the entire module.

Creating Modules

After you create your own functions, you can package them into modules for use in other programs and scripts. Creating modules out of functions that you commonly use may save you a lot of time, as you can just reuse them for future projects. Python makes it very easy to create a module and import it to another program; all you must do is the following:

- Make sure that the file you created the function in is saved in the ".py" extension.

- Ensure that the file containing the function is in the same folder as the file you are importing the function to.

Here's a practical example of how to do that. Let's say we're creating a function that will join multiple input phrases into a single string. The function might look something like this:

```
def args_to_string(*args):
    string_1 = ""
    for i in args:
        string_1 += i + " "
    return string_1
```

We can save the function in a file called argtostring. py and after that, we can create another file in the same directory using PyCharm. Next, we import the function for use.

```
from argtostring import args_to_string

string_1 = args_to_string('Hello,', 'this', 'should',
'be', 'one', 'string.')

print(string_1)
```

While using an imported function in the same directory is that simple, you may have to use a function that is in a different directory. Here's a quick look at how you can access a file that is in a different directory. You can use the sys module, which enables Python to change where it searches for files. Let's assume that the file you created was stored in a folder called PythonPrograms saved on the C drive. In this case, you could simply use the sys module to include that folder as part of the "path," the list of directories that Python will search when looking for files.

```
import sys

sys.path.append('C:\\PythonPrograms')
```

Including these commands in your program would be enough for Python to be able to find the argtostring.py file stored there.

CHAPTER - 10

GAME PROGRAMMING

Now, believe it or not you are almost ready to write your very first game. You already know how to output information to the screen and you also know how to take input from a user.

Well, you can only work on text at the moment but you'll get the hang of it later on. But imagine that with only that know how along with the knowledge of algorithms you can now design your very first game.

We will go over how to design a simple coin flip or coin toss game. We will just go over the design process. The actual programming will follow after the design is complete.

A coin flip or toss represents a certain random element to the results. It's one of those things that you can use to decide how a decision will go.

People sometimes flip or toss a coin when they are not sure what to do given two options.

Why do you have to flip a coin when you can create an app for that?

Now, note that we will not design the graphics for this coin toss game or app. We will only work on pure text. The idea is to ask the user to choose whether a coin will show heads or tails.

You will then make a virtual coin toss. And then display what the result was—either heads or tails. You will then inform the user if his or her guess was right. I bet you can already imagine the Python code that you will use for this game.

Sounds easy, right? Well, there is only one final obstacle (well, two actually) before you can construct this game. You need to learn how to make a virtual coin toss. In other words, how do you mimic the randomness of a coin flip? The other thing is how to make your program choose between two different options—which we will cover after.

Random Number Generators: Mimic a Coin Flip

Now, before we can write a coin flip program, we need a way to produce random numbers. That may sound like something difficult if not impossible. After all, how in the world do you make something random?

Well, the good news is that there is a way for you to generate random numbers with the help of Python programming. As you might have guessed, it requires some really serious math. But don't worry. Someone else has done the math for you.

You don't have to come up with the mathematical formula or the algorithm that will create random numbers. It all has been done for you. In fact, there are several ways to produce random numbers in Python.

We will introduce you to one of these Python language constructs so you can create the coin toss game. To do that we will need to use a function called choice( ). This is only one of several functions in Python that are used to generate random numbers.

Not only do these functions produce random numbers, they can also manipulate the randomness of the numbers being created. In a way, they give you some degree of control so you can decide which set of numbers can be produced.

Note that these functions are used in many games, apps, lottery programs, and many other applications where an element of randomness is needed. They are pretty useful actually.

The choice( ) Function

As it was mentioned earlier, for this coin flip or coin toss game we will use the choice( ) function. So, what is it?

Remember, it is spelled with a small "c" at the beginning. The choice( ) function will output only one random number. That makes things easier for now since all we want is something that will produce either of 2 results.

We can use the choice( ) function to randomly generate either the number 1 or 0—well, we can also choose 1 or 2. It' all up to you which two numbers you will choose. The next question is how does this function work?

Here is an example of how the choice( ) function will look like in a Python program:

```
print (random.choice([5, 4, 3, 2, 1]))
```

You are already familiar with the print( ) function. Next as you can see from the sample above, you use the choice( ) function by using the following line of code:

```
random.choice( )
```

From the said example above you will also notice a set of numbers enclosed within a pair of square brackets, which are the following:

```
[5, 4, 3, 2, 1]
```

This function will choose any of the numbers inside the set contained within the square brackets. Note that only the numbers in this container will be used. That is the control that will be given to you when using this random number generator.

What we have below is called the syntax of a statement. In programming terms, a syntax is the proper arrangement of terms in a programming language so that it can be interpreted correctly (or translated correctly into a language that can be understood by a computer).

The following is the official syntax of the choice( ) function:

```
random.choice([sequence])
```

Here are the parts of this function:

·random.choice – this is the function call or the right way you make use of this function. You need to add the word "random." (followed by a dot) before the word "choice." So you might be thinking what is this "random" part of the statement? Well, that is called the module (we'll talk about modules in a minute). What this part of the code is telling us is that "choice" is part of "random" or contained inside "random."

·[sequence] – this part will contain a sequence of numbers or in the case of our coin toss program it will contain either of two words (i.e. heads, tails). This part of the choice( ) function is the list of items where the output will be selected.

choice( ) is a useful function if you want to specify exactly which numbers will be included in the selection. There are downsides of course. What if you want to choose any number ranging from 1 to 500,000?

Writing all those numbers in your Python code will become way too long if you do it that way. Don't worry. There are other functions that can handle such a task. For now let's just concentrate on using the choice( ) function since we want a limited set of numbers to choose from.

Open your Python console and enter the following lines code:

```
>>> import random

>>> print(random.choice(["heads","tails"]))
```

Import Statement

We used the following statement:

```
>>> import keyword
```

And now you have:

```
>>> import random
```

The reserved word "import" is a statement that is used to import or make use or bring in predefined codes. Don't let that technical sounding thing scare you. This statement makes use of the import system in Python programming.

You remember that it was explained earlier that other people have written the algorithms and the Python code for a lot of tasks that you will need in programming. In this case when you need a program that will generate random numbers, there are others who have already done the job for you.

All you need to do is to use their code. That means someone else already wrote the code for the choice( ) function that we were discussing earlier. Now, in order for you to use that function you need to import it from the code that they wrote into your code.

That eliminates the need to write what they already wrote. All you need to do is to import it. In this case you will import something called "random."

In Python programming "random" is something called a module. Think of a module as a collection of programming code that has already been made for you to use. You have now learned two modules in this programming language—random and keyword.

You can't use the choice( ) function without importing the random module first. That is why you start with an import statement first and then use the choice( ) function.

Now, moving forward—notice that when you press enter after this line of code:

```
>>> print(random.choice(["heads","tails"]))
```

The system will display either heads or tails. Press the up arrow key to display that command again. Pressing the up arrow key on the command console of Python will display the last command that you entered. That way you don't have to retype everything over and over again. This only works on the command line console.

Notice that the pattern produced is random. There is no specified number of times the words "heads" or "tails" will be selected.

Coin Flip Game Algorithm

Now we are ready to create the algorithm for the coin flip game. Here it is:

1.Greet the player and mention the name of the game.

2. Explain the rules of this game: a virtual coin will be tossed. There will be no graphics involved. Just an imaginary or virtual coin toss for now.

3.The player will guess whether the coin will show heads or tails.

4.Flip or toss the coin.

5. The player that guesses the side of the coin gets 1 point, the player who doesn't guess, is deducted to him 1 point. The player who gets 3 points, wins.

Programming Exercise

Judging from the algorithm above, you already know how to perform steps 1 to 4. Open your IDLE editor (or if you have installed a different IDE then use that one instead). Write the lines of code for steps 1 to 4.

You will see a complete coin toss/coin flip program later on as we go over the rest of the game design. There are a couple more concepts that you need to learn so that you will be able to complete coding for this project.

CHAPTER - 11

MORE GAMES

Rock, Paper, Scissors

This classic game involves choosing one of three objects, as the name suggests. Once both selections are made, the items are revealed to see who wins. The player who wins is determined by three simple rules. The rock will crush the scissors, while the scissors cut paper and the paper covers rock.

To handle these rules, we are going to create a list of choices, similar to the list of colors we created before in some of our drawing programs. Then we will add a random selection function that will represent the choice the computer makes. Next, the human player will have to make his or her choice. Finally, the winner is decided with the help of a number of if statements.

Have you tried to create your own version of

the game yet? If so, good job! Even if you didn't completely finish it or you wrote the game and you're getting some errors, you should still reward yourself for trying. Now, let's go through the code and see how this game should turn out:

```python
import random

selectionChoices = [ "rock", "paper", "scissors"]

print ("Rock beats scissors. Scissors cut paper. Paper covers rock.")

player = input ("Do you want to choose rock, paper, or scissors? (or quit) ?"

while player != "quit":

    player = player.lower ()

computer =  random.choice(selectionChoices)

print("You selected " +player+  ",

and the computer  selected"  +computer+ ".")

if player == computer:

print("Draw!")

elif  player == "rock":

if computer == "scissors":

print ("Victory!")

else:
```

```
        print("You lose!")

    elif player == "paper":

        if computer == "rock":

            print("Victory!")                      else:

            print("You lose!")

    elif player == "scissors":

        if computer == "paper":

            print                               ("Victory!")
        else:

            print("You lose!")

    else:

        print("Something went wrong...")

    print()

    player = input ("Do you want to choose rock,
    paper, or scissors? (or quit) ?"
```

Now let's break down the code and discuss each step.

First we import the random package which allows us to use a number of functions that we are going to take advantage of when giving the computer the ability to make random choices. Then we create a list for the three game objects and print the games rules so that the human player knows them. The computer will already know what to do because it is programmed, after all. Next, we ask the player to type his or her choice and then a loop is executed to check the choice of the player. The player also has the option of quitting the prompt window, and when that happens the game is over. Our loop makes sure that if the player doesn't select the quit option, the game will run.

The next step is to ask the computer to select one of the three game objects. This choice is done randomly and the selected item is stored inside a variable called "computer". After the choice is memorized, the testing phase begins to see which player will win. First a check is performed to see whether the two players have chosen the same item. If they did, then the result is a draw and nobody wins. Next, the program verifies whether the player chose rock, and then it looks at the computer to see if it chose scissors. If this is the case, then the rule says rock beats scissors, so the player wins. If the computer didn't select a rock as well, neither did it pick scissors, then it certainly chose paper. In this case the computer will win. Next, we have two elif statements where we perform two more tests that check whether the player selected paper or scissors. Here we also have a statement that checks to see if the player chose something that isn't one of the three possible items. If that is the case, an error message is sent that tells the player he either chose something that he is not allowed, or he mistyped the command.

Lastly, the user is prompted to type the next selection. This is where the main loop goes back to the beginning. In other words, the game starts another round of rock paper scissor.

This game is simple, but it is fun because anyone can win. The computer has a chance of beating you and there's also a real chance of ending up in a draw. Now that you understand how to create a random chance type of game, let's look at other examples to add to our game library while also learning Python programming.

Guess!

This project will be another fun chance-based game that will make use of the random module. The purpose of the game will be choosing a number between a minimum and a maximum and then the opponent tries to guess that number. If the player guesses a higher number, he will have to try a smaller one, and the other way around as well. Only a perfect match will turn into a win.

In this project the random module is needed because of certain specific functions. For instance, we know that we need to generate a random number, therefore we will use a function called "randint" which stands for random integer. The function will have two parameters, which represent the minimum number we can have, as well as the maximum. You can try out this function on its own. Just import the module and then type the following:

```
import random

random.randint (1, 20)
```

Python will now automatically generate a random figure between 1 and 20. Keep in mind that the minimum and maximum values are included in the number generation, therefore Python can also generate numbers 1 or 20. You can test this command as many times as you want to make sure that you are truly getting random values. If you execute it often enough, you will see that some values will repeat themselves, and if the range is large enough you might not even encounter certain numbers no matter how many times you run the code. What's interesting about this function though, is that it isn't truly random. This is just a side note that won't affect your program, but it is intriguing nonetheless. The randint function actually follows a specific pattern and the chosen numbers only appear to be random, but they aren't. Python follows a complex algorithm for this pattern instead, and therefore we experience the illusion of randomness. With that being said, let's get back to fun and games. Let's create our game with the following code:

```python
import random

randomNumbers = random.randint (1, 100)

myGuess = int (input ("Try to guess the number.
It can be anywhere from 1 to 100:"))

while guess != randomNumbers:

    if myGuess > randomNumbers:

        print (myGuess, "was larger than the
number. Guess again!"

    if myGuess < randomNumbers:

        print (myGuess, "was smaller than the
number. Guess again!"

myGuess = int (input ("Try and guess again! "))

print (myGuess, "you got it right! You won!")
```

That's it! Hopefully you tried to create this game on your own because you already have the tools for the job. Remember that programming is only easy as long as you practice it enough on your own. Just take it one step at a time. With that being said, let's discuss the code in case you need some help figuring the game out:

Just like before, we first need to import the random module so that we can use the random number generating function. Next, we use the randint function with two parameters. As mentioned before, these parameters are the lowest number we can guess, which is 1, and the highest number we can guess, 100. The random number generator will generate a number within this range. Once the number is generated, it is stored inside the "randomNumbers" variable which we declared. This number will not be known by the player because he or she needs to guess it. That's the point of the game.

Next up, the player needs to guess the hidden number. This guess will then be stored inside a new variable called "myGuess". In order to check whether the guess is equal to the number, we are using a while loop with the "not equal to" operator. We do this because if the player gets lucky and guesses the number correctly with the first attempt, the loop simply doesn't finish executing because there's no need.

Next, if the player guesses the wrong number, we have two if statements that check whether the guess is a higher value than the hidden number, or a lower one. An appropriate message is then printed for the player in each case. In either scenario, the player receives another chance to make the right guess. Finally, at the end if the user guessed the number correctly, the program declares victory by printing a message and then the program stops running.

To make the game more interesting you can challenge yourself to modify the random number generator to include different values. You can also add a statement that enables the game to print the score to see how many times the player tried to guess the number. In addition, since the game ends when the player guesses, you could write a main loop so that the player can choose to restart the game instead of automatically quitting. Have fun and don't be afraid to try anything.

Choose A Card

Card games are always fun and they also rely on random elements to some degree. No matter the card game, chances are quite small to have multiple identical games. This means you won't get bored any time soon. With what we tackle so far about Python programming; we can create a card game. It might not look good, unless you have an artistic friend to draw everything for you, but you could still create the graphics with the help of the Turtle module like we did for other projects. This will require some patience though. In any case, we can create a card game even without graphics by simply generating the name of each card. Instead of seeing a virtual card, we will see the name "four of spades", or "queen of hearts".

One of the simplest card games we could create involves a game with two players that battle each other to see who draws the card with the highest value. Each player will randomly pull a card from the deck, and the one who has the higher card will win. It is a simple game, but fun due to the random element.

Since we won't be using any graphics, we will have to create our deck of cards some other way. We are going to set them all up as a list of strings since we will be using their names instead. Next, we need to give the players the ability to randomly pull a card from the deck. This means that we are going to use the random module once again and we will add a choice function that randomly distributes cards to the players. Finally, we need a way to compare the two cards that are drawn by the two players. As you probably guessed, this is a case for comparison operators.

That is pretty much all it takes to create a card game. You can add more features, or remove some if you aren't interested in them. Whatever you do, design the game on paper so that you know your goals. Then work one those goals one line of code at a time. This way you will write your game in no time and whatever problems you encounter you will be able to fix fairly quickly.

CHAPTER - 12

HOW TO DEAL WITH ERRORS?

Spot and Fix Errors

The Python interpreter takes in every line and operates on that straightaway (more or less) when you press the Enter key. In hi World! You utilize Python's print feature. Print takes what's within the parentheses and outputs it to the program line (also referred to as the console).

Python is sensitive to each the synchronic linguistics and punctuation. If you spell one thing, the program will not work. If Python is expecting special characters and you do not place them in, then Python can fail. Some Python problems area unit shown here. Are you able to calculate however you'd fix them?

>>> print('Hello World!') Trace back (most recent decision last):

```
File "", line 1, in Name Error: name 'print' isn't outlined
```

Here's another:

```
>>> print ('Hello World!) File "", line one print ('Hello World!)

Syntax Error: EOL whereas scanning string literal
```

Here's another:

```
>>> print 'Hello World!')

File "", line one print 'Hello World!')

^ Syntax Error: invalid syntax
```

Python tries to provide you the rationale it failing (that is, Name Error and Syntax Error).

Check Every Of Those Things:

All commands area unit properly spelled (fail 1)

Every gap quote mark features a matching closing quote mark (fail 2) each gap parenthesis features a closing parenthesis (fail 3)

Using print from Python two versus print() from Python three

The print () that you simply used for your 1st program during this project doesn't would like the parentheses. Python two features a totally different print syntax from Python three. In Python two, print may be a keyword. Before Python three came on, the hi World program was pretty simple and sounded like this: print "Hello World!"

This program doesn't have parentheses. For no matter reason that individuals guilty do what they are doing, the Python software package Foundation modified the Python three syntax to need the parentheses. once you're writing, bear in mind to place parentheses around what you wish to print.

For the code during this book, print can work notwithstanding you allow the parentheses out. (Don't believe me? act. Try it.) as a result of Python 3's syntax needs parentheses, I'm victimization them here therefore you'll be wont to them after you switch to Python three.

Work with Literals

In hi World!, the message that print is causation is named a literal. think about a literal as being one thing inside single quotes. (Single quotes area unit this ' rather than quotation mark, like this ").

Literals area unit the rocks (not rock stars) of the programming world. You'll choose them up and throw them around, however you cannot modification them. they'll exist by themselves in an exceedingly program, however they don't do anything: >>> 'Hello World!'

'Hello World!'

That's a program that has solely a literal and zilch else. It's simply a bit totally different from the hi World program. Therein program there have been no quotes within the text that Python written, however during this example the second line has inverted comma marks around it.

Python doesn't decide the content of a literal, meaning you'll spell it, fill it with weird words, and even fill it with weird, misspelled words. You continue to won't get a mistake message from Python.

The single quotes area unit necessary. If you allow them out, Python thinks the text is telling it to try to one thing. During this example, Python doesn't recognize what hi and World area unit speculated to do: >>> hi World!

```
File "", line one hi World!

^ Syntax Error: invalid syntax
```

The literals mentioned here area unit all string literals. String literals area unit scan like text, rather than sort of a range. (I do not know why they're referred to as string literals and not one thing else, like alphabetical literals.) You'll build a sequence of characters into a string literal by golf stroke one quote on every side: hi World! → 'Hello World!'

However, watch what happens after you build a literal from one thing that already features a inverted comma (like the word didn't) : >>> 'didn't'

```
File "", line one 'didn't'

    ^

Syntax Error: invalid syntax
```

Python reaches the second inverted comma and thinks that it marks the top of the string literal — however that's not wherever you needed it to finish you'll build a literal that has one quote by victimization quotation mark round the outside of the literal. you'll use quotation mark any time, notwithstanding there is not one quote concerned.

> >>> "didn't" "didn't"
>
> >>> '"I have an awfully eely ground-effect machine," he said.' '"I have an awfully eely ground-effect machine," he said.'

Ways you'll produce string literals embody such numerous components as single quotes and quotation mark. however, that is not all! you'll additionally use triple single quotes and triple quotation mark to form string literals. Seriously: >>> '''This may be a literal created with triple single quotes.'''

> 'This may be a literal created with triple single quotes.'
>
> >>> """This may be a literal created with triple quotation mark [sic].""" 'This may be a literal created with triple quotation mark [sic].'

Make sure you'll produce a minimum of one literal that features an inverted comma, one that features a double quote, and one that has each one quote and a double quote.

Literally Save Your Strings in Variables

Okay, therefore you're a master maker of string literals. When Python defines a literal, it kind of forgets it (like you would possibly forget to try to your chores). Python stores literals in memory then thinks they don't seem to be being employed therefore throws them get into a method referred to as pickup. (No, I'm not creating that up.) kind of like after you leave one thing on the ground and it gets thrown within the trash as a result of somebody thinks you are not victimization it. However, does one stop Python from thinking your literal isn't being used?

Put a reputation to your literal. Then Python won't throw it within the garbage. It's kind of like tape a chunk of paper thereto with "Mine!" written on that.

You name a literal like this:

1. Concoct a reputation that follows the foundations (criteria) listed when these steps.

2. Place the name on the left aspect of AN sign (=).

3. Place the literal on the proper aspect of the sign.

Here area unit some of sample names:

```
>>> my_message = 'Hello World!'

>>> my_second_message = 'This name may be a very little long. Ideally, attempt to keep the name short, however not too short.'
```

Each name you utilize should suits (follow) these rules:

It ought to describe what the literal are used for. for instance, text_for_question may be a sensible name for a literal that has the text for a matter (if you're asking the user something). However, another_var may be a dangerous name for it, as a result of it doesn't describe the variable.

Start it with a letter or AN underscore. (Beginning with AN underscore, which is _, features a special that means. you'll avoid it for currently.)

It will have underscores (and ought to typically be manufactured from solely minuscule letters and underscores).

It Will Have Numbers.

It will have uppercase letters (but simply because it will doesn't mean you should; avoid uppercase letters in literal names).

It Cannot Have an Area.

It can't be a similar as any Python keyword. (This project features a list of keywords.)

Use a reputation to visit what you have named. When you utilize a reputation (except on the left aspect in AN assignment), Python acts like you've retyped fully the worth that's documented by the name.

A value is a few things that are documented by a reputation within the earlier examples, the sole values area unit literals. You'll see totally different styles of values within the later comes.

Whenever you provide a name to a literal (or the other value), you're creating AN assignment. In my_ message = 'Hello World!' the worth 'Hello World!' is allotted to the name my_message.

You could rewrite your hi World! program like this:

```
>>> my_message = "Hello World!"
>>> print (my_message) hi World!
```

This assigns the name my_message to the literal "Hello World!" (Remember, the name goes on the left aspect of the sign and therefore the literal goes on the proper aspect of the sign.) Then prints the literal that you simply named my_message.

When you've created a reputation, you'll modification what it names by victimization a similar naming method for a special literal. Or, use another name (since referencing the name is that the same as retyping it). To refresh your memory, this can be the code from earlier within the project:

```
>>> my_message = 'Hello World!'

>>> my_second_message = 'This name may be
a very little long. Ideally, attempt to keep the
name short, however not too short.'
```

Now, bend your mind and assign the second name to the primary name and print it:

```
>>> my_message = my_second_message

>>> print (my_message)
```

This name may be a very little long. Ideally, attempt to keep the name short, however not too short.

```
>>> my_message = 'A third message'

>>> print (my_message) a 3rd message

>>> print (my_second_message)
```

This name may be a very little long. Ideally, attempt to keep the name short, however not too short.

```
>>> my_message = 'Hello World!'
```

Also notice that the worth of my_second_message didn't modification. The sole issue that modified throughout AN assignment is that the variable name on the left aspect of the sign.

You can assign numbers to variables and add, subtract, and compare them:

```
>>> a = one

>>> b = two

>>> print (a) one

>>> print (b) two

>>> print (a+b) three

>>> print (b-a) one

>>> print (a> a = a+1

>>> print (a) two
```

Here, Python appearance up the worth of a, will increase it by one, and then stores it back within the variable.

CONCLUSION

Learning how to get started with computer programing can seem like a big challenge. There are many different programming options that you can go with, but many of them are hard to learn, will take some time to figure out, and won't always do all of the stuff that you need. Many people fear that they need to be really smart or have a lot of education and experience in coding before they are able to make it to the coding level they want. Python has made it so easy to get started with coding whether you are a beginner or have been in this business for some time. The language is based in English so it is easy to read and it has gotten rid of a lot of the other symbols that make coding hard to read for others. And since it is user domain, anyone can make changes and see other codes to make things easier. This kid's book has spent some time talking about the different functions that you can do in Python and how easy it is for a beginner to get started. You will find that this process is easy and you can learn it with a little bit of practice. It is easy to use, works across a lot of platforms, and even the newer Mac systems come with this already downloaded.

When you are ready to get started on programming, or you want to find a program that is going to do a lot of great things without all the hassle, make sure to check out Python. This is one of the most popular options when it comes to programming and you are going to find that it is easy to read and learn, even if you have no idea how to start in the first place.

Working in Python can be one of the best programming languages for you to choose. It is simple to use for even the beginner, but it has the right power behind it to make it a great programming language even if you are more of an advanced programmer in the process. There are just so many things that you are able to do with the Python program, and since you are able to mix it in with some of the other programming languages, there is almost nothing that you can't do with Python on your side. It is not a problem if you are really limited on what you are able to do when using a programming language.

Python is a great way for you to use in order to get familiar and to do some really amazing things without having to get scared at how all the code will look. For some people, half the fear of using a programming language is the fact that it is hard to take a look at with all the brackets and the other issues. But this is not an issue when it comes to using Python because the language has been cleaned up to help everyone read and look at it together. This kid's book is going to have all the tools that you need to hit the more advanced parts of Python. Whether you are looking at this book because you have a bit of experience using Python and you want to do a few things that are more advanced, or you are starting out as a beginner, you are sure to find the answers that you need in no time. So, take a look through this kid's book and find out everything that you need to know to get some great codes while using the Python programming.

Printed in Great Britain
by Amazon